Looking back on 1967
and my time in the U.S. Army.

Like George Carlin used to say
"If you can remember the 60's - you weren't there".

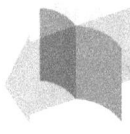

Chapbook Press

Schuler Books
2660 28th Street SE
Grand Rapids, MI 49512
(616) 942-7330
www.schulerbooks.com

ISBN 13: 9781948327284

Library of Congress Control Number:2019910956

Copyright © 2019, Kenneth McKenney
All rights reserved.

No part of this book may be reproduced in any form without express permission of the copyright holder.

Printed in the United States by Chapbook Press.

On November 6, 1967 I was drafted into the Army and went from being referred to as Ken McKenney to eight numbers. Guys drafted had a US in front of their number, the guys that joined the army had RA in front of their number. The men that joined never got any different treatment than the drafted guys.

We traveled by bus to Fort Knox, KY for basic training. The winter was very cold, so we had no outdoor training when it was below 20 degrees F. The food was marginal, and I quickly lost 20 lbs. We were introduced to pneumatic injections. Days were long and grueling and the nights were short. Everyone took their turn at something they called "fireguard", which included keeping the furnace going with what appeared to be a WWII coal furnace. We also had the occasional fire drill which was always in the middle of the night. We were entitled to 7 days leave for Christmas 1967 and flew home for a short 7 days which included travel time, so it was really 5 days. After surviving "Boot Camp" we had a parade for those families that attended the graduation on January 23, 1968. An ideal example of the training technique was how to take a bunch of malcontents and turn them into a team. It seemed like once a week we had PT tests, obstacle courses, and running track times. We would have to pair up and the DI (drill instructor) would have everybody line up by height. Then we split the line in two, with the smallest guy paired with the biggest guy. We alternated turns going piggy-back to the far end of the track, then switched places and ran back. I guess this was their idea of fun. We passed by the famous gold storage building a couple of times while we were there.

The flight from Louisville, KY to Oakland, CA was interesting. Somewhere midway we hit an air pocket and we were all pushing ourselves down from the ceiling for a couple of seconds. It felt like we dropped a thousand feet and I thought the wings were going to snap off when it stopped. We landed in Oakland CA and we boarded a bus from Oakland to Fort Ord, CA.

I did my best to "never volunteer for anything" - rule number one. I was selected as group leader for our bus. My job was to keep track of everybody in our group, 60 guys, every time we stopped. We traveled overnight and stopped for breakfast in the morning. I had a voucher for 60 people and we ate at a place called "Sambos" (almost a copy of IHOP). The bus ride south was what I expected California to look like and we pulled into a military base with a big impressive gate and sign, "Welcome to Fort Ord". The new Company area was more WWII barracks and with a great view of Monterey Bay. Once again we were divided into 4 platoons and each platoon had their own barracks.

Advanced Infantry Training (AIT) was the next dose of Military training. We got used to the new drill - lights out at 11pm - with barracks white glove spotless before we crashed. Reveille was 5:30am and Formation was 6:30am with a roll call. Breakfast was at 7am and a training day started at 8am -

usually until 6pm, sometimes 7pm. Our old M14 rifles were traded for M16 assault rifles. Weapons training included M79 grenade launcher, M50 machine gun (50 cal), M60 machine gun (30 cal). I aced both of these. Also, M9A1 rocket launcher (bazooka).

The food was much better, but not much time for meals. I lost another 10 lbs. More pneumatic injections. We kept our barracks spotless at all times and every Saturday morning there was an inspection. The CO and staff would go through each of the 4 barracks and rate them - 1st - 2nd - 3rd and 4th place. Lunch on Saturday included sheet cake that was excellent and who-ever finished in 4th place had to serve the 1st place platoon their cake. Seemed like a pointless competition but accomplished a great team spirit for each platoon and the company.

We were introduced to M113a Armored Personnel Carrier and half of our training centered around this lightweight tracked vehicle. It wasn't really armored - it was aluminum and underpowered. We made the best of it and Fort Ord and the surrounding training area was a very nice place. There was an area that had moss hanging from the trees, which I had not seen before.

Graduation was March 25, 1968. Most of us would be going to Vietnam but a few guys went to Germany. (I learned years later that this was actually true when I met a guy that went to

Germany for his time in the service.)

I was promoted to Specialist 3rd class (Spec3) and I received orders to go to Fort Carson, Colorado.

I received a weekend pass during AIT at Fort Ord and went to Santa Cruz CA for a Saturday and Sunday. It was a small coastal town with a boardwalk and amusement park that reminded me of Saint Joseph MI. We saw people surfing for the first time. I had a great time with three friends from my platoon. I will never forget the hotel room we stayed in - one of us collected the money and rented a hotel room with one bed. Later in the evening we entered one at a time (we couldn't afford individual rooms) and 15 of us stayed in one room. We drew straws for the bed. We had a great time. I was never sure if the management of the hotel knew what was going on.

I had a flight from Oakland CA to Denver CO and went from the airport to Fort Carson by bus. I was assigned to the 3rd platoon of "C" Company of the 5th Mechanized Infantry Division - (C 1/61). Their ID patch was a simple red diamond like on a deck of cards. The altitude took some getting used to (5,000+ feet). The base was a close neighbor to a giant mountain named Cheyenne and also not far from the city of Colorado Springs.

In training we were once again introduced to more weapons and APC (Armored Personnel Carriers), variations like the self-propelled 107mm mortar and a flame thrower, and also a command unit with communications.

We were introduced to the M60 tank and all of its weapons. We learned how to use the LAW (Light Anti-tank Weapon) which replaced the bazooka, a shoulder fired rocket launcher. Also an aimable mine called a claymore, a fuse that looked like plastic clothesline and called Det-Cord. A plastic explosive called C4 which could be molded and had many uses. A chunk the size of a golf ball could raise a car 4 feet off the ground!

Sometime in April of 1968 we were informed that we were going to be "On Call" for riot duty in Chicago, and had to organize our gear so we could leave in a moment's notice. This was worse than going to Vietnam, I thought to myself, and was a new heavy cross to bear for the remainder of my time at Fort Carson.
FYI: there were 83 people killed and 1,500 injured in the riots that summer plus $100 million in property loss.

We were introduced to the next step in weapons training and learned about artillery support. The smallest was a towable version of the 105mm cannon, a slightly larger version was a 155mm cannon, and a self-propelled version of the 155mm called a Paladin (M109A6). The larger version was an 8 inch self-propelled howitzer (M110)

We went to play war games in May of 1968 and spent about

three weeks in the "boonies" - southern Colorado desert very similar to Arizona. We slept in pup tents, survived a huge thunderstorm with lots of fan lightning. Once on a trip out to the desert training area in southern Colorado we were playing war games and at night I was sleeping on only an air mattress. I woke up in the middle of the night and realized there was some kind of animal at my feet. I couldn't make out what it was in the dark and moved my head to get a better look. It was about 2 feet tall and it took off like a shot. I could see little puffs of dust every 8 feet or so and realized it was a jackrabbit that disappeared in an instant. One other thing I found interesting was there was a variety of cactus and one we saw was a bush 6-8 feet tall, made up of branches about an inch in diameter, covered with thorns. Our track driver ran directly over one once and I looked behind us to see the thing just spring back up undamaged - weird. (We were very careful what we bumped into out there).

My 21st birthday was in June and I was 15 miles from the nearest bar. It was a day undistinguished from the rest of my time there. The one unforgettable thing that happened at this time was that Robert Kennedy was shot and killed.

At the end of May we were informed that the entire 5th Division was going to Vietnam on July 22 and we would be allowed 2 weeks leave in 2 shifts. A lottery was held and everybody drew for either the first leave or the second leave time. I drew the first leave, but a friend in my platoon had drawn the second and was hoping to go on the first leave for personal reasons, so I traded with him. He was a nice guy from Texas, looked a little bit Native American and had a Texas accent.

Another event that I will never forget is the day we had a sandstorm. It was impossible to go outside and it was almost as dark as night for several hours that day. The APC's were all parked in rows at the motor pool and the side of the tracks facing the storm were sandblasted down to bare metal.

We learned that Cheyenne Mountain was home to a top secret underground missile base and was a "no fly zone". Occasionally fighter jets were sent to intercept any trespassers. We went up the mountain and half way up there was a Christmas village. We went beyond just to see what would happen - MP's in a jeep showed up like magic and stopped us. Only authorized personnel were allowed beyond this point, and they weren't smiling.

At the end of my training I was promoted again to Specialist 4th class (SP4). I guess I received a raise in pay also but that was sent to my home in Michigan. I never really needed much money and too much was a good way to get yourself in trouble. Some of our Saturdays we had afternoons off. We went to Colorado Springs and enjoyed places they had to offer that were not off limits to the military. There was a large Airforce Base nearby, so obviously the military had a huge presence in this community's economy.

During my stay at Fort Carson we had our first casualty. A tank mechanic changing a road wheel on a tank had the jack pop out from under the tank and kill him.
I returned to Fort Carson after my leave of 10 days and spent the rest of my time getting ready to go to Vietnam - grateful I never had to go to Chicago for riot duty. The 5th Division was going to fly from the nearby Airforce Base to Vietnam. On July 22, 1968 we loaded everything on the biggest planes I ever saw, called C5A Galaxy - the tail was taller than a 5 story building! We left Colorado and flew to Anchorage, AK. Landing there was an amazing experience. The landing gear had electric motors to bring the giant tires up to runway speed (so no smoking tires upon touch down). The vibration of all of those wheels spinning was nerve racking to say the least. After a short layover there (we didn't get off the plane) we left Anchorage and headed to Yokota Airforce Base, Japan.

We left Anchorage around 3pm and flew about 12 hours to Yokota AFB, Japan. We landed early morning and left the plane for breakfast. All of our gear was off loaded and reloaded onto a C130 Hercules. We left there around noon and headed for Da Nang, Vietnam.

We landed in Da Nang around midnight and the interior lights were switched to dim red lights about a half hour before we landed to adjust our vision to no lights. The ramp at the back went down and there wasn't a light anywhere except a little from the interior of the plane. I stepped off the ramp to what seemed to be large corrugated steel sections - must have been instant runway. As I stepped on it an F4 Phantom fighter took off a mere 60ft away and as it went by us the noise hit us along with a 30 ft blue flame as it passed by at 180mph! Welcome to Vietnam! We thought for a second we had the shortest survival time in Vietnam ever. We grabbed our duffel bags and went to a screened building and found a cot. After my nerves settled I got a very short night's sleep. In the morning I saw my surroundings for the first time and could hardly believe I was awake. Everything as far as the eye could see was covered with red dust - a very strange and hazardous place with trucks of all sizes zooming about. After breakfast we went to an unoccupied area of the base and set about filling sand bags and building half buried bunkers to reside in when absolutely necessary. The heat was way beyond anything I experienced before. In spite of a pretty good tan, I got a sunburn with blisters. After a week to acclimate and adjust to Vietnam, along with learning some of the language, we packed our gear and headed east to a place called Wunder Beach.

We spent the next 3 days filling sandbags and building bunkers. The camp was on a beach of white sand and you could see the ocean (I was told it was the Gulf of Tonkin or South China Sea) in the distance. We stayed there for about two weeks - going on patrol of the area in our 'tracks". Soon we had problems with the sand grinding up the road gear on our tracks and spent more time fixing them than using them. Our brass decided to move to a new location. We did get an afternoon off and swam in the ocean there (someone was on guard at all times). Unfortunately, one of the guys in my platoon stepped on a mostly buried blue bottle jellyfish and was sent to the hospital.

Just a bit of info on medical. Since the day we arrived in Vietnam we had been taking a salt tablet every day to replenish the salt we lost in sweating gallons every day. On Mondays we took a giant pink pill for malaria. (I understand that mosquitoes here are the size of a quarter). Every six weeks we got a booster for one disease or another that was good for six months.

Our next destination was a place called Con Thien (somebody told me it was Vietnamese for rat hole which is appropriate after seeing the place, but the actual translation was "Hill of Angels"). On the military maps it was called A4. This firebase was about 1.5 miles from the DMZ (Demilitarized Zone) and when we arrived there, the current occupants - the 3rd Marines were just leaving. There was a large explosion inside the base and we were informed that the extra ammunitions were destroyed, which was SOP. Later that afternoon the same ammo pad was restocked by Chinook helicopters for our use.

It was called a firebase because of all the artillery and mortar units there. The next day we went on a patrol of the area on foot and were taught how to exit and enter the base camp. The perimeter was made up of a barb wire zone with claymore mines about 100 feet wide and a mine field another 100 feet wide with a maze that was impossible without an explanation. The area definitely looked like a war zone with bomb craters and armored vehicles destroyed by mines.

On the second day there I rousted early and was going on mine sweep detail. This happened every day while I was at Con Thien. We lined up in our tracks behind a special M60 tank with what appeared to be a giant lawn roller. It was a steel cylinder about 10 ft high and 14 feet wide with cleats all over it filled with water. The tank pushed this devise down the road and any mine it ran over just went poof with a puff of smoke - very effective. I went on this detail many times while I was at Con Thien, which was the last base camp on the road north. We went south to a base called the Water Point, next to a bridge that crossed the Dong Hoa River. One of the times we ran across the Red Cross Truck that ran over a mine and was laying on its side off the road. Interesting that sick call was at 6:30 am and the Mine sweep detail was at 7:00 am. I guess you had to be desperate to go on sick call for a day.

On September 18th we went on a mission started by C Company loading on to Chinook helicopters and dropping us (from 10 feet up) on a hill that had a number I don't remember.

It was dusk so we dug in for the night. At dawn all hell broke loose and we were getting hammered with artillery from North Vietnam and 122mm rockets from the mountains west of us. All we could do was call for support that amounted to medivac helicopters coming to pick up the many wounded men from our company. Later I heard that we landed with 189 men and at the end of the day we left 98. That didn't include the 8 bodies that the choppers would not return for because it was too dangerous. The task of carrying one of the bodies was mine and the body was the man I traded leave time with from Texas. We crawled away at night making our way to the creek bed about 1.5 miles away (the military use of meters was never my thing.) I volunteered to go out on a listening post so I didn't have to spend the rest of the night with a dead friend. About 4am we made our way to the top of the next hill and dug in, hoping we were not discovered and that we could have the choppers come back. This was by far the most horrible day of my time "In Country". The most difficult part that I could not get out of my mind was when an artillery shell came down in the foxhole next to mine. The ground shook and something hit me in the forearm and stung for a second and then continued a burning sensation. I knocked it off in the dirt and then realized it was a piece of someone's brain.

Just about daylight we had 3 more rockets come in and not only did they find our position, they had us targeted.
One of the rockets came down about 10 feet in front of me while I had my head and shoulders above ground.

I heard and recognized the sound of the rockets and the next thing I knew I heard someone shouting "Is anyone hurt?" I opened my eyes for a second and saw my foxhole buddy's leg across my lap and soaked with blood - and I thought to myself - wow this guy must be hurt bad. The next thing I knew I was listening to the sound of a Huey and I opened my eyes and was in a stretcher with a medic. Bandages were on my face and shoulder and I realized it was me that was wounded.

Surprisingly, I didn't feel that bad, the medic had already given me something. After reaching a MASH unit I was on a gurney for some time and managed to sit up. Soon a doctor stopped by to check on me and wanted to look in my mouth. He looked around inside and said nothing but got a little scissors and quickly made a couple snips. He took a chunk of metal out of my lower lip about the size of a pencil eraser. He said, "Hold out your hand" and he slapped it in my palm and walked away. I didn't even have time to flinch.

(I still have it in my box of mementos along with some funny money we used in "Nam")

The rest of that day was a blur and the next morning I woke up feeling awful, my face swollen and I couldn't see out of my left eye. A big piece of shrapnel hit 2 of my teeth and broke them off. My mouth was getting very painful. The doctor said it would have to wait for the swelling to go down before they could fix it. After a week they fixed my teeth and most of my wounds were healing, and I was able to walk around some. The wounded men at the hospital were such a depressing time. I soon realized I would rather be back in the war zone. At the end of the second week I got my wish. On my return to the 5th Division I received a Purple Heart (9-20-1968) and my orders for the next mission.

C company went on foot (again) to the east and sometime after noon we crossed an open rice field surrounded by narrow hedgerows. I caught something moving beyond the tree line to my right. What I saw was several men in khaki uniforms coming out of the tree line across the field and the lead man was aiming at our point man. I leveled my M60 and pulled the trigger and mowed the front three down while moving closer to the tree line for cover. To my surprise and shock the tree line beyond erupted in return fire. A few minutes later we seemed to be outnumbered and taking fire from two different directions, pinning us down. Our platoon leader called for support and in what seemed like a few seconds a white smoke shell came down right on us. He adjusted the coordinates and 5 HE artillery shells came down on the tree line beyond ours. We were starting to get incoming mortars from somewhere and the next thing I knew the sound of two F4 Phantoms came from behind us. We watched as they both dropped 500 pound bombs over our head and we saw them fall just beyond the tree line in front of us. Being that close to a 500 pound bomb when it explodes was terrifying - a halo of shrapnel followed with some space, followed by black and orange flames, followed by a huge cloud of grey smoke. The concussion knocked the wind out of me. The incoming small arms fire slowed down after that but the mortars didn't. The fighter jets came around for the second time and fired 20mm beyond the next tree line. As the second F4 was climbing away it suddenly cut to the left and dove into the trees beyond. The remaining one left and didn't come back. I thought that this was not in the script, something was seriously wrong and it was starting to look a little bleak for us. (There was a total of 445 Phantoms lost in the Vietnam War). We held our ground until late afternoon when we were relieved by A Company and made our way back to Con Thien. I wasn't sure how many wounded or killed our company had and nobody talked about it.

The following morning we packed up our gear and left Con Thien in our tracks for 3 hours and saw some amazing country. I saw my first out-door market with animals hanging from the eaves - chickens, ducks, cats, dogs, pigs, monkeys, etc. We had a collection of candy left over from our sundry packs (all the necessities toilet paper, soap, gum, candy, cigarettes, etc.- our platoon got one free every week) and as we passed through a village the kids would come running so we tossed the stuff out to them. Felt good to see smiles again. The candy that survived the tropics well included Life Savers. The other thing we always had was an abundance of fruitcake that came in the C-rations - nobody liked it so we saved it for the kids. One other thing I recall we received was what appeared to be Hershey Chocolate Bars. They looked just like the ones at home but instead of Hershey it said Tropical

Bar. The contents looked like chocolate but you could lay it in the hot sun all day and it wouldn't melt and tasted like a wax candle (I guess it's the thought that counts).

We made our way to a place called LZ Tombstone (there was a graveyard nearby) and this place was not what we expected in Vietnam. It seemed more like the Sahara desert - sand dunes for miles in all directions. So we made ourselves at home (made sand bag bunkers) and there was no place to get out of the sun except our tracks which were more like an oven. If you could have found an egg it would have fried in a second on the hot surface. The first night was clear with a full moon. I was amazed at how the sand seemed more like snow to me and the brightness was a welcome change.

This place was like a prescription for us and the war didn't seem to reach here. We went on patrols with our tracks but the only thing we saw was an occasional puddle which was almost invisible in the sand until you splashed through it. Speaking of water, the water source for us was a small creek with a dam - above the dam was drinking water and below the dam was bathing. We received our replacement men about 5 days later and that meant we were ready to head back to the war zone.

On the way back to Con Thien our convoy hit a snag - the track in front of us ran over a mine and I was looking directly at it when it happened. The explosion was a big grey cloud of smoke and an unfortunate man sat with his legs dangling over the side of the track (they told us to never do that). I saw a leg from the knee down flying through the air. Not an easy scene to forget. We pulled into Con Thien late in the day. Some of the marines were still leaving. A marine helicopter was leaving and just cleared our perimeter when one of the three blades flew off and it wobbled to the ground and fell on its side. It wasn't very high off the ground so nobody was hurt - we had work to do so I didn't get to watch the show. I later learned it was a Sikorsky H19 Chickasaw and it looked antique to me. Whenever I spent the day at Con Thien I went to the mess tent for lunch and had to walk by the 8 inch guns to get there. It seemed that they always waited for me to walk by and the barrel came up above the gravel bank around it and fired it over my head. The explosion would knock the wind out of me and the dirt would jump a foot off the ground. I got to the point where I just plugged my ears every time I walked past there.

We stayed an extra day there getting organized for a mission that would take several days on foot. We were going to a place called the A Shau Valley. We were going with some engineers to stand guard as they blew up a bridge which was a part of the Ho Chi Minh Trail. It crossed a good size river and was made of trees and looked like the one from the movie "Bridge on the River Kwai".

The journey to the valley was uneventful, but getting through the jungle was a whole new experience. It was very rugged and thick jungle with 90 percent of the plants having thorns and 90 percent of the leaves had leaches. We tried everything we could think of but every morning we had to strip and burn the leaches off with cigarettes. About mid-day we stopped for a snack in this creek-bed at the bottom of a gorge. In spite of being a sunny day there was no sun here. I found a big enough rock to sit on and when I did I leaned against a spider web. I followed the web up to an orb web that spanned the creek-bed, in the middle was a spider about 8 or 9 inches across - all black with yellow joints - front legs raised and looking straight at me. I jumped up and was about to say something when the guy next to me with a machete threw it and it hit handle first with a loud clack. The spider flew into the bushes and it hit the ground running and disappeared. I wondered to myself - what else lives in this god-awful place? Later that afternoon I got my first look at a Vietnam jungle centipede. It was rust color with yellow legs and black tips and it was 12 or 14 inches long. I couldn't see the whole critter at once since it went from crevice to crevice. After reaching our destination we set up camp and used our training to clear a landing zone (LZ) for the first time. We picked the only flat spot we could find with an area big enough for a chopper to land and started clearing it with machetes. Next the engineer strung Det-Cord (looked like plastic clothes line). They wrapped it three times around the bigger trees and went from one to another - 10 or 12 trees and set up a detonator. We went to take cover a good distance away and the explosion sheared off the trees level with the ground. We hauled them off to the side, leaving a nice wide open space in the forest. The next morning a chopper came with supplies, mail, and all the gear that the engineers needed to complete their mission. I couldn't see what they were doing, but they set about putting charges on the bridge and we enjoyed the lull of a non-stressful day. We stayed one more night and the following morning there was the biggest explosion I had heard yet - again I didn't get to see it but we heard them say "Yup, it's gone". We headed back to Con Thien and I thought to myself - "God I hope I never have to come back to this place again".

While I was helping clear the LZ I mentioned earlier I was using a machete and chopped down what looked like a large fern, about 6 feet tall with spines on the leaves and toothpick size thorns on the back. I stomped it down and was about to move to the next bush when it popped back up. It was about to hit me in the face so I stopped it with my hand. (Big mistake) The thorns went almost through my hand, and after pulling them out of my hand the punctures were surrounded by green goo. When we returned to Con Thien I went to see the medic and showed him the wounds on my hand. They looked better but my wrist was breaking out with blisters. He gave me some clear ointment to put on it which made it go away in a couple of days. (For the next 10 years, every time it got hot in the summer, I got these little blisters on my wrist.)

We spent the next two days at Con Thien and on the second day coming back from lunch I heard the familiar sound of a 122mm rocket come down someplace in our base camp. My instinct said run for it - I ran across the road to the perimeter bunkers and dove head first through the door and there were two explosions. When I thought it was safe to look out I saw a crater where I had been standing when I heard the first one. All I could say was "Thank You God".

The next day about late morning we got word that A company was in a fire fight to the west and we got orders to go help them ASAP. We packed up our gear and left in our tracks. It started to rain and we crossed several creeks on the way to their location. We got there late in the day and the rain was beyond belief. When we arrived the battle was over so we dug in for the night. Early the next morning I woke up and realized that I fell asleep in my fox hole and It had filled to the top with water. Startled by this, I jumped a little which only made it worse. I was cold and wet and crawled out of the hole and came face to face with an emperor scorpion about a foot long - not knowing that they're not that dangerous. I freaked out and grabbed a log nearby about the size of a baseball bat and bludgeoned the thing to a pulp. My platoon leader came over laughing and said you OK? I said "Ya I am now - God I hate this place". Since we were no longer needed here, we headed back to Con Thien. Even though it only took about 4 hours to get there, we spent 3 days getting back. So, this was the monsoon season we had heard about. One of the little creeks we crossed on the way out was now a mile across. Even though our tracks were supposed to be amphibious, it was our first experience of swimming our tracks across deep water. The 2nd platoon didn't do so well - they managed to sink one of their tracks in the middle. Somebody had to dive and attach a cable to retrieve it. The track survived nicely but the guy's belongings not so well. We had several occasions where our track got stuck and with the help of a cable we kept moving - at one point we had 3 of them cabled together. One of the times we were stuck on a berm surrounding a rice paddy and they hitched a cable to give us a tow. I rolled off the back without looking (the water was only 2 feet deep) and realized that one the deadliest snakes was swimming away right under me. I freaked out and jumped away and fortunately the snake was swimming away fast. They told us that there were 30 different kinds of snakes here, all very deadly. Staying put was not an option - if the cable broke it would take your head off. Once more I thought to myself "Thank You God".

We returned to Con Thien and we all had dishpan feet. Con Thien was made of red dirt and the next 3 or 4 days we walked in red mud up to our knees. We had the Company of Marines join us and they had some M60 tanks that filled the empty spots in the perimeter. I had an aluminum folding cot that I used outside (too hot and too many critters inside the bunker - spiders, centipedes, scorpions, and rats). I was sleeping next to one of their tanks when in the middle of the night the tank started firing its main gun. To my amazement they had some kind of auto-loader and the 109mm empty shells were dropping on me. Lucky for me the mosquito netting saved me from a solid hit. I couldn't get back to sleep after that so when the barrage stopped I talked to the marines about the auto-loader, which we didn't have on our M60.

I guess it was our duty to check out "Leatherneck Square" every now and then so we went out on a patrol on foot again. It was always a little nerve racking to work our way through the maze and mine field at Con Thien, and we were half way out when mortars came down in the base camp somewhere. One of the enemy saw us leave and knew where we were headed. An hour or so later, walking on patrol, we had two mortars come down near us and one of them landed about 4 feet from me with a thud, but didn't go off. I froze and wondered do I dare move? The engineer in our group said, "back away soft and slow". They put a claymore next to it and at the end of the wire, blew it up.
Once again I thought "Thank You God".
Without further incident we made it back to Con Thien. FYI, of the hundreds of mortar shells I saw come down, this is the only one I knew of that was a dud. They told the new guys to stick by me in the boonies - I had some kind of magic aura.

The next mission was in our tracks again and we headed east toward a base camp called A2. We were in more open country and our tracks were quite spread out when something happened, and I wasn't sure what was going on. The 4th platoon's command track had purple and orange smoke coming from it, and we never heard anything. Evidently a mortar landed right in the track and killed everybody. The smoke was for choppers to identify the smoke color - they were all burning. More mortars came down and they were trying to hit more tracks. Somebody thought they heard the thump of a mortar launching and so we opened up in that general direction.

Small arms fire came from the right and directly in front of my machine gun, so I was firing 10-15 round bursts into the trees there. A little right of me was an M60 tank. A shoulder launch rocket stuck out of a bush and fired directly at the tank. When the smoke cleared the tank had a scratch in the paint. The 109mm was aimed in their direction and evidently loaded with a canister round (large shotgun shell). They pulled the trigger and the bushes and its occupants disappeared as if by magic! The next thing I realized was that my machine gun had run away - when I released the trigger it just kept on firing. I let it finish the 100 round belt (the 5th one so far today). The barrel was almost translucent red and I got out my asbestos glove and exchanged a spare barrel and reloaded. At that point there was a deafening roar and an F4 flew over and dropped a 500 pounder in the trees beyond us. Shortly afterward another F4 flew right over our head firing 20mm with a short burst and 5 or 600 rounds erupted off to the right of the bomb burst. The next thing I realized it was raining 20mm casings on us - 2 hit me on the steel helmet which I was glad to be wearing. I wasn't aware that the empties came out of the plane, and was thinking we just took some incoming fire - and I said to myself again, "Thank You God".

We also had a couple of Huey Cobras show up and they finished the job with dozens of rockets. On the way back to

Con Thien I checked on my barrel and it had seized up into a solid. I thought it would make a good boat anchor. When we got back I was elected to clean out the track and restock the ammo - boxes stacked two layers deep covering the floor of the track. I was in the process of moving the cans (large metal storage boxes) and moving them outside the main door on the back so I could clean all of the debris on the floor, including empty shells. I reached out to grab a handle on a box and when I moved it the biggest centipede I ever saw crawled across my hand. I yelled and jumped 3 feet back out of the track. Did I mention that the critters were as bad as the war?

A couple of days later we set off on another mission. This time we were on foot again and I was getting really tired of hauling a 23 pound machine gun and 200 rounds of ammo, plus all of my gear, so I started cutting back on C rations. I had an assistant gunner who also carried 200 rounds for me. The standard drill for patrol on foot was that there were always 2 and sometime 3 M60 machine gunners on a patrol. When crossing open ground I would find a high spot and cover everybody as they crossed open ground. The next gunner would do the same and so on. We were crossing an open rice field and my partner was covering us. I made my way to the front of the patrol so I would be ready for the next open space. We were going through a thick hedgerow that somebody cut an opening through with a machete and the lieutenant and his radio man got in front of me. My assistant gunner was in front of them going through the hedgerow. Our patrol was 2 lines of men about 30 or 40 feet across and 10 or 12 feet from one to the next. As the lieutenant crossed through somebody hit a trip wire and an explosion went up just to the right of me, about 60 feet away. When the smoke cleared the grass I was standing in was flattened and somebody was shouting "medic". The lieutenant and his radio man were killed and my assistant gunner lost his right arm at the elbow. Men behind me were down with wounds, and also on the right. Somebody ran for the 2nd platoon for a working radio and called for a chopper. Our platoon leader had been with us since Fort Carson CO and was a tough blow for us to lose.

While standing in the blast circle I realized that the only thing that happened to me was my eyebrows were gone - I was still standing, and nobody could explain it. So again I thought to myself, "Thank You God". We made our way back to Con Thien and the next morning we packed up our tracks and went to the next base camp south, which was called C2. We had passed through there on the way north. This base camp had an artillery battery of 155mm self-propelled howitzers. The perimeter defense was antique-looking rocket launchers on tripods called 90mm recoilless rifles. We got a demonstration to fire this weapon. You stand off to the side (never behind) and pull the lanyard. The rocket inside the tube shoots a 20 foot flame out the back when it is fired. Impressive, but I thought It was way too big of a target to fire it at night. We stayed there for a couple of days and then moved north to the Water Point and stayed overnight. The bunkers were way too full of critters so I just laid down on top of one and went to sleep. I woke up in the middle of the night with a giant rat sitting on me...no more sleep for me! The next morning we had a day off and were allowed to swim in the river. To do so, the procedure was to toss 2 grenades off the bridge into the water, it was then safe to swim for about ten minutes. (There were fish that must have been related to piranha and they could take a nip out of your leg if you weren't careful). I came out of the water with the biggest leach I'd ever seen, but overall had a great day.

The next morning we packed up the tracks and went back to Con Thien. We met our new platoon leader who seemed like a nice enough guy, from New England. We left for a couple of days at the ocean and went past our old base camp at Wunder Beach. It must have been high tide and with the monsoons the guard towers and gate were sticking out of the ocean. I could hardly believe it was the same place. We all got to swim in the ocean again and the ghost crabs were fascinating.

On the 2nd of November they stopped bombing the DMZ and we saw the B52's many times dropping long strings of bombs. Our next patrol (on foot) was to the area where the bombing was going on. We crossed a river to get there and I covered everybody as they crossed holding on to a big rope. I was one of the last to cross and the rope had stretched so that when I got to the middle it was over my head. I was pushing down on the rope while trying to hold a 23 pound machine gun over my head to keep it out of the water. I wasn't sure I could make it - had a real struggle. When I got across I thought to myself, "Thank You God". We worked our way through some thick jungle and we heard a shot from the shotgun the point man carried. He shot first and asked questions later. He shot a mountain lion (didn't know they had those there). We continued on and the jungle was thick and dark until we came upon a place that seemed like walking out on an expressway. All of the foliage was laying on the ground and the trees were bare - quite a shock. We trudged on across with the soggy foliage up to our knees. We later learned that this was a common practice and aircraft sprayed the jungle with a defoliant called agent orange. We continued on until we came to the place where bombing had taken place and walked along the edge of some of the bomb craters big enough for a house to fit in. When I was walking along the top of a bomb crater my leg slipped down underneath the dirt up to my knee, and I quickly pulled it back up. There was foliage underneath and my leg was covered with giant ants. Not as freaky as spiders or scorpions, but almost. I brushed them off and continued on my way. We spent the night in the forest and I rolled up in a poncho - in the morning it was raining and there was a little stream running under me. We got up and made a little coffee with some C4 (burns like sterno) and headed back. On the way back we ran across another bomb with a trip wire someone discovered without setting it off. We set up a perimeter around the engineer, who rigged it for destruction.

We heard someone yell "RUN" and we did just that. About 10 seconds later there was an explosion that almost knocked us down. Shrapnel went through the trees above our heads and leaves were falling on us. I thought to myself, "Thank You God." The rest of the patrol was uneventful and we made it back to Con Thien.

The next morning we went out with the mine sweep detail. When we got back there was another mission for us and we were going to leave the next day. I was on guard duty until midnight and someone called in "movement in the barbed wire". I looked through my twilight scope and could see movement out there. The OD came back on the radio and said south side open fire!

I fired my machine gun, there were also M16's and M79's, (grenade launchers) and a couple of 50 cal's, and also some 60mm mortars. Quite a spectacular show that lasted about ten minutes - ceasefire was called and that was the end of the excitement. In the morning we went out on foot to investigate and what we found was at first funny and then sad. We had wiped out a herd of warthogs - the area looked as if a bulldozer was at work.

So off we went in our tracks - we were on our way to the mountains to a place called Camp Caroll, a large fire base south of Kason. On the way there we took some sniper fire that came from a pagoda. One of our tanks without hesitation vaporized the beautiful structure. A little while later we had a tense moment when an RPG rocket hit our track right above the engine. We had a raggedy hole but no harm done. A Huey solved the issue for us and we continued on. (Later on the mechanics put a big plate with bolts over the hole and we got the nick-name Frankenstein for a while.)

We reached Camp Caroll and the view was spectacular. We were only going to be there a couple of days and since the place was already occupied we dug foxholes between the established perimeter positions. More red dirt, only this time every other shovel full had a scorpion in it. The critters here (Vietnam) seemed almost as big a battle as the war. That night I saw my first "Puff the magic dragon" and it was only a couple of miles away. It was a solid red line coming from the sky to the ground accompanied by a sound that was something between a roar and buzzing. I was glad it was on my side. The next morning we went on a patrol and the area was tough going - no flat ground here - and the heat was oppressive. We had a couple of guys pass out from heat so we headed back. I didn't think it was possible for a place to be worse than Con Thien. This place definitely gets the trophy. I saw a group of men that looked Vietnamese but were very dark skinned and almost looked like Indians from South America. They were called Montagnard and carried cross bows and were on our side.

We headed back to Con Thien and came across an M60 tank that had run across a mine. The road gear was gone and the tank was sitting on the ground. In spite of the damage, nobody was hurt (except for their hearing). We stopped to cover the area and waited for their rescuer. A little later this machine that looked like a cross between a tank and a giant wrecker showed up - an M88 tank retriever. They hitched up some cables and off they went dragging a 60 ton tank with no wheels - I was impressed. We made our way back without incident. We spent the next day at Con Thien and I was walking to the mess tent for lunch when an explosion above us knocked me down. I got back up and realized I wasn't hurt but exclaimed (like everybody else) "what the hell was that?" Later that afternoon we heard that it was what they called a "short round"; a 16 inch shell from the battleship New Jersey, somewhere just beyond the horizon (we could see the ocean from Con Thien). At night we could sometimes see large fiery donuts out to sea and too far away to hear any sound. The next morning we had 2 F4's only a half a mile from us dropping HE and napalm - I got some great pictures but was worried about how close it was. This morning I went on the mine sweep detail. We had an M60 tank with us - we went south to the Water Point and turned around to head back. My friend driving the tank said he would switch with me and I got to drive the tank on the way back. As big as it was I was glad I didn't have this as my job - just a little claustrophobic, but seemed like driving an office building on a narrow road. Glad I got to try it anyway.

Thanksgiving was coming up next week and we heard that we were going to stay put at Con Thien and have a "turkey dinner with all the fixins". I had visions of Norman Rockwell and anticipated something spectacular. It was delivered by Chinook helicopters and we looked forward to this. It seemed like most of the time we ate C rations. When we first got here the C ration cans were dated 1945 and came with 4 cigarettes. If you lit them sometimes the paper would catch fire, so they were more dangerous than new ones. Most of us just threw them away because they were also unfiltered with brands like Lucky Strike, Pall Mall and Camel. That old stock seemed to be gone. The C rations now, even though they looked the same, were dated 1968 and were not as good as the vintage WWII ones were!

The Thanksgiving dinner was served early afternoon and a tray was delivered to me, as I was on guard at the perimeter. The turkey was tough and stringy and stuffing was gritty. The gravy was thin and everything was cold. I was disappointed but glad to have something that didn't come in a can. I thought to myself, "Thank You God".

The next morning, we got orders to go back to the A Shau Valley and help the engineers blow up a bridge again. So we left on foot and made our way to the same place as last time. I also received orders that I was to transfer to a new unit and head south the end of the week. I asked my platoon leader if I was supposed to go with them. He said "you're kidding, right?" Off we went to the same bridge, to my astonishment - it's the same bridge! How is that possible? It was only six weeks ago we were here and blew this bridge up. The good news was the LZ was still usable and we didn't have to make a new one. I needed to report to my new duty the next day, and it was a 2 day hike back. After the engineers blew the bridge I went back to the hill next to the LZ and had lunch. I was in an ugly mood and was angry. While I was sitting on the ground a huge grasshopper came and landed on me. I'd seen these many times, so I brushed it off and didn't pay attention to where it went. A few seconds later it came back and landed on my leg again. I knocked it off, annoyed, and watched as it flew away, circled around, came back and landed on me again. This time I grabbed it and threw it to the ground, pulled my Colt 45 and blasted it - a three inch hole in the dirt where it used to be. Several guys came running, thinking there was a problem and I explained the situation to them. They walked away chuckling.

Just a few minutes later the chopper came with supplies and mail and the right door gunner turned out to be my replacement. I hopped in behind the gun mount, the M60 was just like mine and off we went back to Con Thien. I packed up my gear in my duffel bag and hopped in a 3/4 ton Dodge pickup (M37) and we headed south to the airport at Quan Tri. 2 hours later I was at the airport and boarded a C130. When I got on the plane there were no seats - you had to sit on a big aluminum pallet and hold on to a cargo net that looked like seat belt material. The C130 went slowly to the end of the runway and turned. Then backed up so the whole tail section was off into the weeds - is this a normal thing? It revved up the engines full blast and the whole plane shook and roared. The pilot then set the props and we lunged forward quickly, gaining speed. A few seconds later the plane leaped forward with a huge roar, a system called JATO (jet assisted takeoff), and the back of the plane went down with a crash. We were dragging on the runway for a second and then the plane shot up on a steep angle, clearing the trees at the end. The pallets we were sitting on all went bang-bang-bang to the back of the plane. There wasn't a calm looking face in the bunch of us on that flight. 2 hours and 500 miles later we landed at a coastal city called Qui Nhon. I got in the back of a deuce and a half and headed west and inland. The ride was uneventful and actually beautiful country with farms and villages and no more jungle anywhere. We went to an Army Base and the sign said 184th Ordnance Battalion - Prov Guard. This was a huge step up from anything I had previously seen in Vietnam. There were sidewalks, barracks, landscaping, and paved roads, and a PX with an NCO club.

I met my chain of command and was issued new clothes. I had a new set of jungle fatigues and boots stored in my duffel bag (it looked more like it was buried). They were unsalvageable. The barracks had screened walls but real beds, and what luxury. I had a great night's sleep and was up early and went to the mess hall for breakfast. The guy running things was from my old unit, and we became great friends. The rest of the day was a tour of the base - a tour of the ammo base 3 miles down the road west. Our post had only a barb wire fence and lights with no guard towers. We had a few sand bag bunkers. The main defense was a couple of WWII self-propelled twin 40mm anti-aircraft equipped tanks called a "Duster".

Half way between our post and the ammo base was a place they called the brass yard and there were mountains of brass shells of all kinds. The ammo depot was at the bottom of a steep valley covered with jungle (I knew it had to be someplace). The next day we joined up with a group of guys that were the perimeter guard at the ammo base. There were large towers (about 30 of them all together) and additional barbed wire outside. Beyond that was a mine field with more claymores. Guard duty was 4 hours on and 4 hours off, and then 4 hours on again for a 12 hour day. That left 8 hours to sleep, and 4 hours of free time! The army must have slipped up here and I thought to myself, "Thank You God".

Guard duty during the day was a little boring. It was more interesting watching ammo trucks coming and going; also front end loaders moving about the ammo pads. There were approximately 30 ammo pads with huge gravel banks around 3 sides, with the open side facing a paved road. The trucks seemed to be a contract outfit from Korea. They brought in all kinds of ordnance, from small boxes to 8 inch artillery shells, 6 to a pallet. So for the next 2 weeks I did guard duty and when I was at the post, the mess hall there served three meals a day. The first time I was on guard duty early in the morning at the ammo base the jungle around the base was surrounded by howler monkeys. They started whooping at first sign of daylight and continued sometimes for almost an hour. What a din, sometimes it could get on your nerves. During the day with binoculars we saw no sign of them anywhere.

The sergeant that managed the main gate for the ammo base (there was only one way in and out) turned out to be an old friend from the 5th Division who was wounded and never came back to our platoon at Con Thien. After recovery he came here to Qui Nhon. When he received orders to leave he must have recommended me for his replacement. I was summoned to see the Base Commander of the Ammunition Base Depot. I stood at attention in front of a Full Bird Colonel and he said "have a seat". He explained that I was being promoted to sergeant and was going to be in charge of the main gate. My job would be taking two guards back and forth from the post, 7am, and 3pm, and 11pm. Between 8am and 12pm, I would be checking on guards in the towers. I received a new uniform and a helmet that looked like an MP but said SG. So I went to meet the men (gate guards) back at the post. This was an unexpected turn of events and was most welcome.

I soon learned the job and looked forward to going back and forth to the ammo base in a jeep. During the day it was a piece of cake job. The 11pm trip was not so fun and I drove the biggest thing I could get, which was a 5 ton truck. We would go as fast as I could with the 2 guards in back manning a machine gun. Every 2 or 3 days someone tried to hit us with mortars. Of course they never did or I wouldn't be writing this story. But it was unnerving having a huge flash just off the side of the road. I would have a meeting every Friday morning with the Colonel, and we became friends. One day I was at the gate when a truck driver stopped. I noticed he had a WWII grease gun in the seat and asked where he got it. He smiled and said "it's yours for $50". I added it to my arsenal, my Colt 45, which was all I had to travel back and forth in a jeep with during the day trips. It used the same 45 cal ammo as the pistol so I could get more without questions. It was a comfort to have it under the seat of my jeep, and being a black market weapon didn't bother me at all. Periodically the perimeter was allowed to test fire weapons (usually at night). We could open up and watch tracers going everywhere. There was a twin 40 "Duster" just to the right of the gatehouse and it fired 320 rounds a minute, so it only fired for 3 - 5 second bursts. This seemed intimidating enough to me that the enemy would stay far away from here (ya right...) I fired my M3 grease gun a few times and the thing almost shook my teeth loose. It had a 30 round clip and was not very fun to fire all 30 rounds; but it was a lot more impressive than a pistol.

The next couple weeks were almost boring and not much happened of interest. I would hang around the gatehouse after the 11pm guard change. The five of us would chat about things like where we were from and what we were going to do when we got home from "Nam". One night we were chatting and we heard a "clang" and a sound like a golf ball hitting the pavement under the gate lights (big poles with giant light reflectors on either side of the gatehouse). Upon inspection, it was a beetle that hit the reflector and fell down (I didn't think things like that flew in the dark). We all went to check it out and it was at least 3 inches long, with pinchers another half inch. Someone grabbed a pencil and teased it a little and "crunch", it grabbed the pencil and almost chomped it in half. A couple of minutes later a second one did the same and when I left the guys were trying to get them to fight each other. Not much else to do there in the middle of the night. After I would leave to go back to post with the guards it was very rare to see traffic on that road at night.

The next exciting thing for me was when I went to check the guard towers. It had been raining hard for most of the night and things were muddy with deep puddles. I went in my jeep to go around the perimeter counter clockwise. It was gradually uphill all the way around, and then a steep hill back down to the gatehouse. I took my time and chatted with each guard and it was 11:30 am. I could go back to the post for lunch, and when I got to the top of the hill I thought about going back the other way around. I put it in 4 wheel drive and creeped over the edge and started creeping down the hill. Half way down it started sliding and turning the wheel didn't seem to matter. About 3/4s of the way down I went sideways on the left side of the jeep facing down the hill (not good at all) and I was watching the mud pile up on the wheels going sideways. It looked like I was going to roll over any second. I made it to the bottom and almost got stuck but straightened it out, thinking to myself, "Thank You God". I got back to post and parked the jeep in the motor pool and they asked "what the hell happened?" I said, not a problem - I didn't get it stuck. The wheels on the driver's side looked like mud balls and the rest of it was covered in mud also.

On a Friday afternoon I was able to find a guy to cover me for Saturday afternoon. I got a pass to go to downtown Qui Nhon and the next day hopped a ride to town. I was aware of the bombing incidents they had downtown so I avoided all the bars with "Purple Haze" blasting out of them and just went touring with a friend (not a good place to be by yourself). We went into a restaurant and had a coke and some dessert. When we left I went out first and was squinting at the bright sunshine. 5 little boys not much taller than my belt surrounded me and had their hands all over me, then vanished, along with everything in my pockets! Live and learn - I must have looked like an easy target and I lost 40 dollars of funny money and my military ID. On the way back to post I decided to grow a mustache and if my next military ID had my mustache on it - it was allowed. Just an FYI - the funny money was changed without warning every 3-4 months or so to stymie the black markets. I had a good time seeing the sights around Qui Nhon. The beach there was beautiful with the small catamarans with colorful sails and umbrellas, and looked tourist-friendly. Quite a surprise considering it was still part of the war that was going on.

Every Saturday night at dark we had a movie we could watch. There was a basketball court we used for karate training and no chairs - we just sat on the cement which was noticeably warm on a sunny day until long after dark. The movies were 35mm reels that came from the States someplace - it was a great break no matter what the movie was. I had my guard shift change at 11pm so I never got to watch one all the way through. One time we started to watch a movie and only 15 minutes in we were hit with mortars and ran for cover. Nobody was hurt - but no more movie either. We had a dayroom with a couple of pool tables and a ping-pong table and some board games. This facility was sort of taken over by an ethnic group that had medical deferments and never had to work, so nobody else could ever find a table open (day or night). Another interesting thing on our post was the showers. There was a separate building from the latrine (toilets) and the roof was a giant bladder of this black rubber-like a tire. This was filled with water and there were no hot and cold faucets. Just off and on, so if you wanted to take a shower there were 10 shower heads in a big room. The temperature was perfect from 5 or 6 in the morning until about 10am, when it started get uncomfortably warm. By 6pm it was around 180 degrees - hot enough for coffee or tea, but not drinkable!

One night I was coming back with the guards from the ammo

base. When we left we could see an orange glow in the direction of our post. We were worried that there was a big problem. As we got closer we could see orange flames and black smoke rising up in the sky. As we reached the front gate we realized that down the road about a half of a mile there was a storage facility across the road. It had a huge tank for gas and another for diesel fuel, and one of them was burning. We learned that this was a common occurrence which happened every 5 or 6 weeks. The war here was not gone, just a lot sneakier. We also heard that the enemy sometimes managed to sneak into the ammo base and insert charges or start fires. I thought this place looked impossible to get into, but evidently they had secret tunnels. The ammo base was almost a total loss a couple times in the past.

It was mid-March and I was going to take the guards out for the 7am shift and couldn't find one of the guys. I looked around the area and thought maybe he was in the latrine, so I checked the sidewalk between the two buildings. I found him half way laying on the sidewalk passed out and reeking of booze. I bumped him with my foot and got a mumble - left and went to report to the officer of the day (OD) that I needed a replacement. He said "you'll have to do it - but I will see to him" and so I left and went to the gate. I left one guard and said "be right back" and took the two back to our post and then returned until about 2:30pm. I had to go back to get the next shift. I called the Colonel's office and let them know I would not be able to make my rounds this morning and they said no problem. The Colonel had an aid that was a sergeant major and he said he would go with the guys that brought hot coffee or soup to the towers. There were also guards with dogs that walked between the towers at night, but that is another story. When I returned to get the 3pm guys they said the other guard was in big trouble, was arrested, and was going to get court martialed. Off we went back out to the ammo base. That evening when I took the 11pm guys out I half expected to get some incoming - mortars or something. Nothing, and we were grateful - we chatted a few minutes and then I took the guys back to post. We were tired and it was a long day for me. After dropping the guys I took the 5 ton back to the motor pool, about to call it a night. Somebody came out of the ODs office and shouted "Red alert at the ammo base". Standard procedure for me was to be at my post (ammo base main gate) during a red alert. It was too late to get a vehicle so a minute later there was 2 deuce and a half with guards heading there so I yelled "how bout a ride?" The man in the cab of the first truck said to hop in the back. They stopped just long enough for me to climb on board, and off we went. This was new to me and I wasn't sure what was going on, but assumed they would stop briefly at the gate so I could jump off. When we got close to the gate I got ready to do just that but we went flying right on through. One of the gate guards blew his police whistle but was ignored. I yelled for them to stop and let me off, but nobody was paying any attention. So back into the ammo base we went - all the way to the back of the perimeter, and turned around. Everybody was getting off the trucks. I stepped on the ground and caught what appeared to be a supersonic shock wave coming from the ammo pad on our left. The next thing I knew I was shaking my head and spitting dirt. I was face first in the gravel bank about 15 feet away from where I stepped off the truck. Quickly I gathered our situation and realized what was going on and looked up. There was a mushroom cloud (the biggest I'd ever seen anywhere) going up at a frightening rate. The man next to me was badly injured. I grabbed him under the arms and started dragging him toward the trucks and yelled "everybody back on the truck". As soon as we were all aboard, including several wounded, we headed out to the main road. As we passed the front of the ammo pad that blew up we saw a tangled mess against the far side of the road that looked like it used to be a jeep. Two seconds later, gathering speed - the truck shook with a crash. I looked at something that went to the side of the road as we passed. It looked like the front fender of our truck, but we made it to the main gate. Quickly forming was a line of vehicles also leaving. An order to abandon the ammo base must have been given. I hoped somebody would stop and pick up my guards. We made our way back to our post and by the time we got there we saw 2 choppers coming our way. The LZ was across the street from the main gate, so the trucks stopped there. While on our way back I was feeling some pain in my left ankle, but it was too crowded to check it out. When I jumped down off the truck I felt a sharp pain run up my left leg and fell down. I realized now that something was wrong. The side of my boot had a big gash in it. Soon a medic came to check on me and got a scissors out and snipped the shoe string on my boot. He took it off and then my sock, which was soaked with blood. I looked at the inside of my left ankle and saw a piece of bone sticking out of a hole. He put a bandage on it and asked "can you hop to the chopper with my help?" "OK", and when I got over to it there were already 2 stretchers and I sat on a bench seat with another medic. Off we went to the hospital at Qui Nhon. I thought to myself, "Thank You God".

The hospital had real buildings, not like a Mash Unit like last time. So the doctors patched up my ankle which was bigger than a football, I kept ice packs on it for a couple days. The next day I woke up and realized there were 5 people standing around my bed. One was a nurse with eagles on her collar and I thought - "jeez, do I salute or what?" Then I noticed they were all brass and one guy was my Colonel from the ammo base. He said, "just relax" and asked how I was doing. "OK except for my ankle". He said something to his aid (Mr Sergeant Major) and he gave him a long blue box that I recognized immediately, as I already had one. I was sort of in a sitting position and he pinned a purple heart on the smock I was wearing and said "we are grateful you made it back". I explained how I was there and not at my post and he said, "don't sweat it". He said he had somebody to cover for me and to take it real easy and would see me in a couple of weeks. I had been writing to my folks once a week and I wrote to tell them I was OK. I thought to myself "Thank You God." A few days later I had to get walking with crutches, and had to walk the halls of the hospital. This was a most depressing place to be and I couldn't wait to get back on duty so I wouldn't have to see any more of the horror. It was crushing to see so many men missing limbs and worse.

After a week I wrote my folks again on my progress and said I was getting around on crutches. Just before I left to go back to the 184th I received a letter from my folks. They received the second letter first and were worried and wondered what had happened. I went by truck again back to my post and when I got back there was mail waiting for me, including a large can. I often got goodies from my mom and aunts. The brownies were the biggest hit and I had a lot of friends every time I received a coffee can! I opened this one and noticed the date was several weeks prior. There was a loaf of home-made bread wrapped in tinfoil, and when I unwrapped it, I discovered a fuzzy green block which used to be home-made bread. I thought to myself, "It's the thought that counts", and chuckled.

The next day I reported to the Colonel and he said that I had 10 days leave coming and I could go on R&R. The choices were either Bangkok, Thailand or Sydney, Australia. Most guys picked Bankok and came back with VD. No Thanks. I picked Sydney and was going to have a fabulous adventure.

I went back to the Qui Nhon airport and took a C130 with a real seat to an airport with commercial airlines, I forget just where it was. (Cam Rahn Bay maybe?) We flew in a commercial airline from Vietnam to Perth, Australia. It was about 14 hours and we flew over Borneo. If there were buildings there they must have been hidden under the trees - nothing but jungle for 2 hours. Later on I looked out the window and saw some whales and from up there it was like seeing fish in an aquarium! We landed in Perth, Australia and had a 2 hour layover, so we decided to have an Australian beer - Fosters. So my friend and I (He was from Michigan and a town called Blissfield) had the beer which was really high in alcohol. I couldn't finish it - the only beer we could get in Nam was 3.2% and this stuff was 12% or more. We left for Sydney and I was looking forward to seeing the view on the way but fell asleep. I didn't wake up until 4 hours later and missed most of the view. We landed in Sydney and had to spend some time adjusting to all of the jaw dropping gorgeous ladies that we hadn't seen for over a year. We got in a cab and went to a pre-arranged hotel downtown in an area we were told was called King's Cross. First thing we did was go to a department store and our group (about 50 GI's) all bought 2 outfits plus shoes. It was a pleasure to have street clothes on again and I bought some light weight western style boots that were perfect. It turned out that the "western look was all the rage" there in 1969. We spent the rest of the day (Friday I believe) exploring our area on foot. When we were coming from the airport we saw a big building with "Bowling" on the front and thought it would be fun to give that a try. Sydney in 1969 was called the city of fountains and there were amazing fountains everywhere we went. There were familiar restaurants there and right next door to our hotel was a "KFC", so we checked it out for dinner. The next day we went to the waterfront and saw the brand new Sydney Opera House - most amazing place. We decided to take a Hydro-foil over to see the Sydney Zoo and Botanical Gardens. The boat ride was exciting but pricey and we didn't realize we'd been had. We had a fabulous time at the zoo and also the Botanical Gardens. After making our way to the far side of what we thought was an Island we saw cabs everywhere; a cab ride to King's Cross was less than half of the boat ride. Oh well - live and learn. That evening we had tickets to go on a harbor cruise and dinner was included, also music and dancing. We went aboard the ship and realized that almost all 50 of us were going on the cruise. Not long after we boarded we realized there were more girls on board than guys (no kidding). Dinner was great and afterwards we paired up with two ladies that said they were sisters. We had a great time and danced and got to know them. They both had jobs downtown and worked Monday thru Friday. So we made plans to spend the day with them on Sunday. We went to see some of the highlights, including many fountains around town - so beautiful. There was a big park that had a very European looking fountain with giant horses in the middle, and a more contemporary one of stainless that looked like a giant dandelion. We went to an upscale place for dinner with silver serving trays and waiters wearing tuxedos with towels over their arm. Everything was excellent - looked like something from a movie set. We had a date to see the girls on Monday night after work, also Tuesday and Friday.

Monday morning we left the hotel to go check out the shopping area and when we got down to the sidewalk we were amazed. The downtown area looked like any other big modern city up to this point. We looked around and the streets were full of carts and people, and no cars! I guess we really were in a foreign country. Monday was shopping day and everything you could imagine was available, some were on a push cart with big wooden spoke wheels. Fresh fish, fruit, vegetables, chicken, bread assortments etc. (Sorry - no monkeys) We took a cab to where the building was that said bowling. When we pulled up in front the nice green lawn between the street and the building was covered with seniors in white suits enjoying lawn bowling. OK, we had to come up with plan "B". We went to a beach north of Sydney and watched the surfers (sort of). The beach was crowded – it was close to April, summer was winding down there.

Monday evening we met the girls for dinner and went to a club I thought was a little bit loud for conversation but the wall had mirror alcoves with "Go-go dancers". Very enthralling, and we had a good time and a little too many drinks. We hoped the girls would be OK for work the next day. We went back to our hotel and they walked home, so they must have lived nearby. The next day we went exploring again and would see the girls after work. I think they both did some kind of office job and had dresses on when they showed up. We went to a restaurant on the bay for dinner and the view was fantastic - the Sydney harbor bridge at sunset. The harbor area was always bustling with boats of all kinds and sizes, including freighters. After dinner we went clubbing and saw 2 more places that were not that unusual, but we had a great time with the girls. Called it an evening much earlier which was OK with us. The girls had a busy day tomorrow. The next day we decided to find a tour bus and do a complete circle to see the most we could of Sydney. We saw a lot of aborigines. They seemed to like to wear bright colors and with their blueish-black skin were very striking. Seniors with their white hair were even more so. We went by a restaurant with a glass front and in the window saw a stuffed "giant red kangaroo". We asked about it and found that they were getting rare to see in the wild. A stuffed one would have to do, I guess. We saw wallabies at the zoo and Tasmanian devils, koalas, wombats - all of the animals we expected to see in Australia. We saw an exhibit that said platypus, but he must have been sleeping or hiding because we couldn't find it. Getting back to the tour, we stopped to have lunch at an old fashioned malt shop with black and white tile floors and round seats that turned. They had cheeseburgers and fries and I thought this was a really cool place to enjoy. We each ordered a cheeseburger and fries and a coke - and it was even better than we expected. I asked for some ketchup for my fries and they looked at me puzzled and said what's that? The tables all had bottles of malt vinegar on them which sounded disgusting to me, so we just ate them plain. We continued on our journey and Wednesday and Thursday were on our own. The girls were going to join us Friday evening for dinner and more clubbing.

On Friday we joined up with girls and had dinner with them. Afterwards we went to a club that wasn't anything unusual but the music was good. We went to another place that was crowded and was "Country" theme - a lot of the folks here were wearing western stuff and everybody had boots. We saw a hat or two, but not a necessary option I guess. The music was live and I recognized some of the songs. I did my best not to laugh, but hearing country songs with an obvious Australian accent was hard to get used to. I was never a big country fan but we had a fabulous time. We went back to the hotel and the girls came with us and we showed them our hotel room. I was thankful to have a tidy roommate. We watched some TV and chatted for a while - we had a room with two bedrooms. When it was getting late and I expected them to go home - they said they planned on spending the night. What a great idea - I had a girlfriend back home and I thought to myself (I better omit this part of the adventure).

The next morning we slept in and made plans for the day. We went to a park on the waterfront and walked around to an area where there were more vendor carts. Somebody was selling hot dogs, so we had lunch at the park. Watching families with kids and a group sailing model boats on a pond - it was like a dream I didn't want to end. We had to head back to Nam on

Monday. We had a fabulous day and we still had Sunday to go but it seemed to be rushing by way too quick. We went back to the hotel and the girls stayed the night again. Sunday was bittersweet - we did our best to enjoy the day with the girls but it would be the last time we would see them and they knew that, too. We went out to a restaurant for dinner and afterward we said our goodbyes - too sad to go back with us, the girls left the restaurant and went home. The next morning we packed up our stuff and took a cab back to the airport.

The flight from Sydney to Perth was 5 hours and I saw the "Outback" this time. It was, except for a couple of lakes, 4 hours of desert landscape. We flew from Perth back to Vietnam. We were allowed to wear our "civvies" back to the 184th Ord. Reaching my post (not much had changed) I checked in with my friends and spent the rest of the day recounting my adventure. The next morning I got a jeep and went to the ammo base to report for duty with the Colonel. The ammo base was a hubbub of activity and back in business. There was a lot of construction equipment still restoring the base and evidence of damage from the last blowup. I heard that the base burned for three days and was declared a no fly zone. This happened every two or three months from what I heard. Wondered what that cost the USA. I had to wait for an hour for the Colonel to return so I could speak to him. I briefly told of my adventures and he said "welcome back", and I thought to myself (I almost didn't come back). He told me what was going on and that I would be back to my normal duty tomorrow. He also said that he thought I deserved a bronze star for the "pad 64 incident" and recommended me for one. "Thank you, sir" and he replied "Thank you Sergeant". He knew my name was Ken and that most people called me "Mac" but he always called me sergeant. I thought to myself, "Thank You God".

Things were back to normal for me for a few days and then we received word that the ammo base was going to have an inspection. MACV Command was coming to the 184th Ordnance Ammo Base. We neat and tidied the best we could and heard of the process and drill to expect. There was a General in the group named Abrams. I was expected to greet and salute him and respectfully ask for his lighter, (they're not allowed inside the base) and thank him. His jeep would be the only one stopping at the gate. On the day of inspection I was at the gate with my two guards and soon the parade came down the road - must have been ten jeeps with tall antennas all flying flags. The first and last jeeps were military police, the second jeep had 4 stars on a red flag. Each jeep had several people and several flags. I had my dress up type uniform for this special occasion and was wearing my Prov Guard starched fatigues with a blue ascot and rope braid. Earlier when I went to the armory to get my pistol, there was a group of men in formation who must have just arrived from the states. On my way out to my jeep they snapped to attention and saluted me... not knowing what else to do I saluted them back and left to go to the Ammo Base. It seemed that everybody was as nervous as a cat that day. The General's jeep pulled up and stopped - I stepped out to greet him and saluted saying "Good morning sir, I need to ask for your lighter if you have one sir". He offered a zippo to me and said "thank you sergeant". "Thank you sir" - and he left and I watched as the whole procession went into the ammo base. I went back into the gatehouse and showed the guys the lighter which had a very ornate crest on it. We waited for almost 2 hours before they returned and the General's jeep stopped on the way out. I gave him back his lighter (he didn't smoke) and I said "have a great day, sir". He smiled and said "Thank you sergeant". They all headed back in the direction of the post. I imagine the general and his staff had choppers waiting for them at the LZ. As the jeeps drove past one of them had my CO in back and he gave me the thumbs up - so I guess everything went smoothly. I never saw so much "brass" all at one time. I thought to myself, "Thank You God".

Nothing unusual happened for the next several weeks - every day was the same. (Military seemed to have a term for every occasion and this was known as SOSDD) I stopped by the CO's office on a Friday morning and he told me I was going to be part of an awards ceremony that would be held in the company area back at the post. He said he would be there to give me a citation, but not a bronze star. The Lieutenant in charge of the detail on March 23rd (who I never saw) took all the credit for getting us organized and evacuated to safety. I heard that there were 8,000 rounds of 155mm artillery shells that went up and that an unexploded shell took the fender off the truck (fortunately not the wheel). I said "I'm so glad to still be alive that I don't care".

The following Thursday was June 17th. It looked like everybody on post who was not on duty at the ammo base was there for an assortment of promotions and ribbons etc. So when it came to my turn the Colonel came out to where I was standing and handed me a very ornate looking folder. Inside there was an official looking certificate. He saluted me and I returned the salute and he said "Thank you, sergeant" and that was that. The Lieutenant worked for the CO or Captain in Charge of the post and was my CO until I was put in charge of the main gate at the ammo depot. It was probably unusual for someone not to have a "chain of command". I just answered to the Colonel in charge of the ammo base. So I checked the award document to see exactly what it said. The certificate looked very impressive and it said -
"Certificate of Achievement is awarded to - Sergeant E5 Kenneth E. MKenny (should be Kenneth P. McKenney)
who distinguished himself by exceptionally meritorious achievement in Qui Nhon Ammunition Base Depot, Binh Dinh Provence, Republic of Vietnam. "During the early morning hours of 23 March 1969 - he arrived at the Ammunition Base Depot where an enemy force of unknown size was expected to attack. When notified of a penetration of the perimeter near Tower 15 he was deployed in that area knowing enemy satchel charges could ignite an ammunition pad at any time.

During this operation Pad # 64 exploded with a high order of detonation wounding several men. He was extremely helpful in assisting the evacuation of personnel to safe ground with a minimum of casualties. His actions are in keeping with the highest traditions of the military service and reflect great credit upon himself, his unit, and the United States Army". Albert E. Hunter, Brigadier General, USA Commanding."

I chuckled when I read "with a high order of detonation". This explosion was possibly one of the biggest ever in South Vietnam - the mushroom cloud went 3 miles up in record time - and burning debris fell a mile down wind.

When I returned from R&R I started a "short timer's calendar" and each day I would mark off the day. I had only about a month left of my 365 and was getting hopeful to make it all the way to the end of the calendar. I met a couple of guys from my old unit, 1st brigade - 5th Mech Division. It was also called the "Red Diamond" or "The Red Devils". They said it had no changes they knew about - they were still in the Con Thien area. Just a FYI, the 5th Division was started in WW1 and continued during WW2 and is over 100 years old.

With 30 days left to go all I wanted to do was keep my head down. I decided to go downtown on a Saturday one last time with some buddies and we had a good time. We wound up staying to curfew, which was 9PM. A deuce and a half truck would pick up guys and bring them back to post. I jumped in back with 2 other guys and the 2 guys in the cab were MP's.

They drove through town blowing their horn. If you missed the last truck it wasn't likely you would make it to the next morning. The truck had an M60 mount in back and no one manning it so I jumped in the spot. By the time we got back to post it was getting dark and I thought to myself, "Thank You God". I didn't want to take a chance like this again.

One day when I was at the main gate, a friend driving an army 10 ton tractor trailer came in the gate and we chatted for a while. I wondered if he could give me a driving lesson - he said "no sweat", so we traded places and I drove this rig around the block. The trailer had a full load and it was a monster with way too many gears. I was thinking about all of the vehicles I was able to drive while I was in the service and it was fun to add this to my list. I started with the M113 APC and then M48 tank, M60 tank, army jeep, 3/4 ton truck, deuce and a half truck, 5 ton truck and now a 10 ton truck. There was also a strange truck at the ammo dump they called a mule, that was a platform with wheels and a small motor. I told my friend about my "grease gun" and that I needed to pass it on to somebody before I left. He said he would take it for $50 and I gave it to him with 2 clips of ammo.

Many times since I started this job at the ammo base I would come back to post after the 11pm guard change and drop off the 5 ton truck, stop by the mess hall, and see if my buddy was still there. I would stop for a visit and he would make me a BLT sandwich that was better than most of the things they served there, and I loved it. One of the first times I went there my buddy said "Hey - come and check this out". We went to this door in the kitchen that went to the storage room and he whipped open the door and turned the light on. There was a brief flurry of activity and I said "what was that?" He laughed and said that it was cockroaches that seem to vanish. That was amazing - we went to check around and it was rare if you could find one. I told him about the 3 inch ones I saw in the jungles up north. Speaking of bugs, I had an incident that was a mystery to me the whole time I was at the main gate at the ammo base. Once a month or so 2 guys would come to the gatehouse in a truck. They got out wearing a white protective suit with head cover and clear plastic face guard. They would put on backpack sprayers and sprayed all around the gatehouse, inside and out. I couldn't help but wonder what they were spraying for (they never told us) and why we didn't need protection from whatever it was they were spraying. They never asked us to move - they just sprayed everywhere and left. We did have a night when termites (the winged variety) came like a plague. By morning they were all laying on the ground at the end of their life expectancy I guess - very weird.

There was another incident that I will never forget also. Most of the time at the main gate there was little to do and it was very boring. I stopped at the gatehouse for the 11pm change and the guards getting off duty were busy doing something. I asked "what's up?" They said that a mouse was in the gatehouse and they were trying to get it. So I joined the search. They had a foxhole shovel they were trying to smack the mouse with. Every time they swung the shovel it made sparks in the dark. I thought to myself, the critter will die of fright. After about 15 minutes I said to the guards getting off duty that we should go. (The guys at the motor pool couldn't leave until I came back with the truck) I never did know if they got the mouse or not.

I had about two weeks left to go and I would go to Cam Rahn Bay where everybody went to process out and go back to the "States". One of the officers tried very hard to persuade me to sign up for 6 more months in Vietnam. I thought I was pushing my luck to stay even one more day than necessary.
I recommended one of the existing gate guards to take my place. He would be promoted to sergeant and take over the job I did. So the time passed without incident and I said all of my goodbyes and packed up my stuff and went to Qui Nhon airport. Once again I boarded a C130 and flew to Cam Rahn Bay. From the airport, I went to a processing center where mobs of guys were in lines for all sorts of things. I found the appropriate line and checked all my paperwork. They checked through my belongings and some guy sorted through all my pictures and confiscated about half of them, saying they were classified information. They did a thorough job of checking for things like souvenirs - nothing belonging to the government was allowed - especially ammunition of any kind. The next group of inspectors checked our uniform (which was

required to leave Vietnam) and some guys hit a snag with inappropriate tattoos, and some had to have a military haircut - no exceptions. Finally I got through all the red tape including making sure my medical was up to date (shots etc.) We went single file to an outbound holding area which was rows and rows of benches that were a single board suspended by posts about chair height.

There was an officer that read us the drill and he emphasized that the list was going to be read over a loud speaker about every 2 to 3 hours. If you missed your name it would be put on the end of the list. So if you use the latrine, have a buddy listen for you. If you fall asleep and miss your name - you'll be here for days. They had flights all around the clock and that included 1 or 2 in the middle of the night. So I stayed awake the first night and listened every time they read off names. Usually they read 120 to 150 names at a time. I listened all the next day and I asked if I could see where my name was on the list. They looked and said we don't have that list yet - probably tomorrow. Not daring to go to sleep for fear I would miss it, I stayed awake all night again. Fortunately there was a window where we get drinks, and snacks or a sandwich. In the middle of the morning they called my name and I thought to myself, "Thank You God". I followed the line to a bus that took us to a plane that said "Continental Airline". I was so grateful to sit in a comfortable seat. We were in the air in a few minutes and I realized for the first time in a year that the most dangerous thing I had to worry about was the flight itself. No more possible mortars or sniper fire or anything like that. I felt like a huge weight was lifted off me. I fell asleep until we landed in Tokyo, and we had a 2 hour layover. I went to a camera shop for my brother, who wanted a SLR camera. It was about a third the cost it would be in the States. I enjoyed walking around the airport and marveled at the sights. Not speaking or reading Japanese, I steered clear of getting lost at the Tokyo airport. So back aboard, we were on our way to Tacoma Washington, USA. It was July 24, 1969 and we left on a Saturday and flew a short time before it started to get dark. I fell asleep again, and when I awoke it was getting daylight out. I looked at my watch and it was only about 6 hours or so - what a short night! The flight was 16 hours total. About two hours after daylight they broadcast live on the PA system the return of Apollo 11 and the astronauts that went to the moon and back. I realized that this was something I would never forget.

We landed in Tacoma WA and went to a military base there so we could process out of the military and go home. I still had 4 months to go, but because I survived a whole year in Vietnam I was able to get out early. Also, those who wanted to could have a steak dinner with anything they had for your request except alcohol. So after I went through the whole processing out routine, I went to a special mess hall. It was a genuine restaurant with beautiful wait staff and the meal was perfect. The steak was twice what I could eat.

I grabbed a cab to the gate and security wouldn't let us leave, I wasn't sure why. It was about 6pm at that point and we walked back to a PX that had an eating area and waited. They said somebody would be in touch when we could leave. I thought it was a bit strange that we were not allowed to wear our dress uniforms home. A military police guy showed up about 11pm and said we could go to the airport then. So we waited for a cab to return and got to the airport about 11:30pm, learning the last flight to Chicago was around 10pm. I still hadn't caught up on sleep from this ordeal, and I also had jet lag. Now we had to spend the night at the Tacoma Airport - lovely (that's not what I really said). In the morning I was thinking about my future and all of the options I had. I considered that I was at a crossroad and could go anywhere and do anything. At this point I was really tempted to go to Denver, CO and start a new life there. My family and my high school sweet-heart were foremost on my mind, and I stuck to plan A. Later that morning we got a flight at about 7:30am and flew to Chicago. We got a connector to Grand Rapids MI and landed about 3pm. The Kent County Airport was familiar and seemed like home at last, and I thought to myself, "Thank You God".

One last point of interest, I recalled the next day several men from Cam Rahn Bay bragging about how safe it was there and that they never saw any action there... While looking at the news there was a report on 3 soldiers shot and killed by snipers in Cam Rahn Bay, Vietnam. Also, the delay at Tacoma

Airport was due to a bunch of demonstrators against the Vietnam War. They left the airport about 10:30pm. The military didn't want us to cross paths because even though we were wearing our civies, we were obvious GI's. It was roughly 10 years before I was able to talk about my experiences in Vietnam. It was a very unpopular subject and a few idiots gave us all a bad name. Now days if you ask a high school graduate what the Vietnam War was, they don't have a clue as to what you're talking about.

In retrospect the whole thing was a mistake and a fiasco. But I served my country with honor and made it home safe, and I still say, "Thank You God".

www.ingramcontent.com/pod-product-compliance
Lightning Source LLC
Chambersburg PA
CBHW050045080526
44586CB00014B/1460